CLB 1707
This 1991 edition published by Crescent Books,
distributed by Outlet Book Company, Inc, a Random House Company,
225 Park Avenue South, New York, New York 10003.
© 1987 Colour Library Books Ltd, Godalming, Surrey, England.
All rights reserved.
Printed and bound in Hong Kong.
ISBN 0 517 62363 3
8 7 6 5 4 3 2

ACADIA
NATIONAL PARK
and
MOUNT DESERT ISLAND

CRESCENT BOOKS
NEW YORK

This is the forest primeval. The murmuring pines and the hemlocks,
Bearded with moss, and in garments green, indistinct in the twilight,
Stand like Druids of old, with voices sad and prophetic,
Stand like harpers hoar, with beards that rest on their bosoms.
Loud from its rocky caverns, the deep-voiced neighboring ocean
Speaks, and in accents disconsolate answers the wail of the forest.

No one ever described it better than Henry Wadsworth Longfellow.

He was describing an area down East, even of Maine, in Nova Scotia, a land once known as Acadie. But the words would have suited just as well for an island across the way, not far from where the Atlantic Ocean meets the Bay of Fundy, which was called Mount Desert by the French explorer Samuel de Champlain, who gave it its name in the 16th century. Not as poetic as Longfellow, Champlain chose to describe it as an island of wild and desolate mountains. Both were accurate, but to Longfellow's heroine, Evangeline, it was "the home of the happy." To the great explorer, it was just another piece of territory to claim for his king.

Even the king thought it worthless, but it was territory to possess, after all. In 1613, a pair of French Jesuit missionaries named Pierre Biard and Ennemund Massé sailed up the Atlantic coast in search of heathen to convert. When they got into far northern waters, they became hopelessly lost in the fog when, after having been adrift long enough to begin contemplating giving last rites to their crew, the sun suddenly came out and they found themselves in the shadow of Champlain's desolate mountains. They found them indescribably beautiful and decided right away that the beams of sunshine were a sign from God that He wanted a mission established on the side of that mountain.

They accommodated Him by building the first Catholic mission in the New World north of Florida and east of California. They called it Saint Sauveur. In no time at all, they had converted dozens of Indians and knew for sure that God was smiling. But they weren't smiling down in Virginia. Samuel de Champlain notwithstanding, the English colonists, as well as *their* king, had decided that the east coast of North America was to be English and not French. The theory had not been tested up to that point, but five years before the Pilgrims set foot on Plymouth Rock, Samuel Argalls, Admiral of the Virginia Navy, went up to Mount Desert and burned the mission to the ground. The survivors of the one-sided battle were loaded on the ships and carted off to the Caribbean to be sold as slaves. It was the first of many confrontations between the British and French in this part of the world.

Argalls claimed the island for England, of course, and a few years later the Puritans from Boston tried to make it profitable by establishing a trading post there. But the Indians, who didn't understand their brand of religion, nor their language, nor their attitude, wouldn't trade with them. The French, meanwhile, were lurking around the area, and the Puritans, who didn't have a taste for geopolitics anyway, closed up their store and went home to Massachusetts.

They still thought they owned it, though. So did a French noblewoman who had bought the place from one of her compatriots who said he owned it. The King of France, meanwhile, disagreed with both of them and gave Mount Desert to Sieur Antoine de la Mothe Cadillac, who settled the argument by moving there to establish his own little kingdom. He didn't stay long and soon went west to establish a little colony he called Detroit.

Cadillac brought a large number of servants with him when he migrated from France and when he left Mount Desert to go west, many of them stayed behind to become fishermen. Mount Desert Island remained a French colony, in spite of what they thought down in Massachusetts, until the British took Quebec in 1759 and the French gave up their dream of an American empire.

The first Englishman to take up permanent residence was Samuel Soames, for whom the

Previous pages: Frenchman Bay, viewed from Cadillac Mountain and (facing page) Somes Sound.

village of Soamesville was named. He liked it there because of the peace and quiet and incredible beauty. But though it stayed peaceful and quiet and beautiful, it wasn't lonely for long before he had plenty of company in the form of other rugged individualists like himself who moved up from Massachusetts and New Hampshire to get away from the bustle of civilization. They became farmers and fishermen and in their spare time they built boats. It wasn't long before fishing and farming were the spare-time activities, and for a long time the Maine coast produced more wooden ships than any other place in the world.

One of the reasons was those murmuring pines. The British shipbuilders had managed to strip all of their colonies all over the world of pine trees tall enough to make masts for their ships. Reforestation was unthinkable, and the tall trees of Maine were discovered just in the nick of time. Not only were the forests thick with them, but the coast was laced with inlets and rivers that made it easy to get the big logs to the ocean.

The only problem was that the people who lived there thought the trees were very nice for making houses. To disabuse them of that notion, the Crown passed an edict that any tree more than two feet around could not be cut by any private citizen. The King's men put their mark on all the forbidden trees and warned the locals that cutting any of them would bring a £100 fine, or worse. It made the British Navy safe from the homebuilders. At least until 1776.

But neither was able to cut all the trees and places like Mount Desert Island remained the most heavily forested part of the United States east of the Pacific Northwest. Their future was secured when the steamship *Savannah* crossed the Atlantic in 1819. The need for houses in Maine dropped dramatically at about the same time. Wooden ships were a thing of the past, and there are only so many rugged individualists willing to live the harsh, if peaceful, life along the Northern coast.

But there was a new industry in the air. In 1794, a man named Jabez Ricker bought a piece of land not far above Sebago Lake. He shocked his neighbors by renting rooms to strangers in his house. He even served them meals, and soon folks were coming all the way from Boston to sample his hospitality. His house eventually became a real hotel, which he called the Mansion House, and passed from father to son and then to Jabez's grandson, Hiram. Hiram suffered from dyspepsia, which wasn't too terrific for a restaurateur, but he discovered it was eased when he drank the water from a nearby spring. His grandfather had served the same water at the Mansion House, but never touted its curative powers. Hiram did. He even bottled it and sold it, which lured more tourists to the source at Poland Spring, and Maine became a destination for vacationers.

Most agreed it was worth the trip, but it surely wasn't an easy trip. Finally in 1824, the steamship *Patent,* which was described as "elegantly fitted for the comfort of passengers," began regular service between Boston and Portland. Two decades later, the service was extended to Bangor, and during the summer months there were waiting lists of people wanting to experience the overnight trip.

A few months before the first boat arrived in Bangor, a well-known painter, Thomas Cole, arrived on Mount Desert Island. On that day, in September 1844, the character of the island began to change. Cole was the founder of a movement among painters known as the "Hudson River School." In the mid-19th century the country, which was beginning to industrialize, was gripped by a back-to-nature movement. Cole and his followers gave the country what it longed for in the form of romanticised paintings of the landscape in the Hudson River Valley. When it was beginning to look as though the market would never be saturated, Cole decided the subject matter had been and began searching Northern New England for new ideas. Mount Desert was his idea of perfection and he settled down.

His enthusiasm knew no bounds and whenever he went back to New York, the Maine coast was his only topic of conversation. The combination of his enthusiasm and his paintings made many of his wealthy patrons interested in seeing the place for themselves. Many of them agreed with him, and most couldn't wait to do more than just see it. Most of them already had elaborate summer places in Newport, Rhode Island, but it was getting crowded down there. Besides, it didn't have the exhilarating combination of forest and sea that Mount Desert offered. And these men, though largely the perpetrators of industrialization, were as much a part of the back-to-nature movement as anybody.

For the first several years, the super-rich went up

from Newport and stayed in homes which enterprising locals had opened up to them. It was perfect for everybody. The people who lived there had a new source of income and their visitors got a nice taste of the simple life. But when you're super-rich, living the simple life isn't always so simple. While it was fun to eat home-made bread and sleep under hand-made quilts, there was no place to do any entertaining on the island. And what's the point of being rich if you can't show off to your friends?

Soon they began building homes in the style that made Newport so opulent and inviting their friends up for occasional dinner parties. There were dozens of such estates established in the last years of the old century and by 1900, Newport was beginning to look to its laurels. But there was a difference in Maine.

The houses were as elaborate, the estates as vast and the State O'Mainers, whose inbred independence made it anathema to them, provided a good supply of servants. But most of the summer people, though conscious of their social obligations, still longed to commune with nature. Many of them solved the problem by building log cabins in the woods, hidden away from their ostentatious houses. Whenever they could break away from the social whirl, they retreated, in secret of course, and never more that a few hundred yards from a hot bath, to find the "natural life." They spent their days gathering seashells or flowers to press. They became avid birdwatchers and agreed among themselves that "green thoughts in green shade" was about as close as a person could get to heaven without dying first.

It had another important advantage over Newport: its remoteness kept the riff-raff out. The only way to get there at first was on that boat to Bangor and then a long horse and carriage trip down to the island. A bridge had been built in 1836, so there was no way to stop anyone from making the trip out to the island from Trenton. But when automobiles threatened to make the trip easier, they outlawed cars. The ruling stuck until 1913.

Railroads made getting there a little more fun, but not much. The most popular train was the *Gull,* which left Boston's North Station bound for Nova Scotia every evening except Saturday. (Nova Scotians didn't like the idea of trains roaring through their Province on Sunday.) The train was comfortable, but if a passenger wasn't careful to start out in the right car, they might wind up in Aroostoock. In deference to sleeping passengers, the *Gull* shed cars as it went north.

But those with the time and the money and the stamina, there was no place on earth quite like Mount Desert Island. Oh, one got a little tired of the same faces all the time, even if they were Rockefellers and Morgans, and communing with nature for an entire season could be tiring, even if there were balls and dinner parties to break the monotony. Everyone coped, and for the most part everyone had a wonderful time. But they all agreed that the best of all the seasons at Mount Desert was the summer of 1914.

America hadn't involved itself in the war that had just begun in Europe, but impounded a German ocean liner bound for New York that spring. She was escorted into Bar Harbor where she remained all summer. Though some of the passengers made the rest of the journey by train, many opted to stay aboard. They had paid for a boat ride to New York after all. Suddenly the Mount Desert establishment had some new playmates, and they were wealthy Europeans at that. The little log cabins in the woods didn't get much use that season.

The following spring, when the British liner *Lusitania,* carrying 128 Americans, was sunk by a German submarine, it was obviously only a matter of time before U.S. neutrality would end. It put a damper on the 1915 season, which many agreed was the end of the road for Mount Desert Island. The war was only one of the villains. Henry Ford was another. In 1914, he raised wages in his automobile plants from $2.40 for a 9-hour day to $5 for an 8-hour day. Fortunately, he spent his summers at Cape May, New Jersey, so there was no one to tell the servants.

When they did find out, most of the houses on the island were put up for sale. Some became schools, others inns, still others were simply abandoned. But there had been a movement afoot since 1910 that would insure Mount Desert's future.

In addition to being a playground for the rich, the island was also the center of a thriving lumber industry. Arguing that cutting trees would destroy the very thing that made the place so attractive, George Bucknam Darr and Dr. Charles Eliot began soliciting funds from the summer people and were able to raise enough to buy 15,000 acres, mostly on Cadillac Mountain. Then they turned around and offered it to the Government as a gift. It wasn't until 1919 that the gift was accepted, and the first National Park east of the Mississippi River was established the same year. At first they named it Lafayette National Park, but in 1928 it was renamed Acadia. By then, the area had grown to 27,860 acres with the addition of more land across the bay on Schoodic Point and out at sea on Isle au Haut. All of the land was donated and given to the Government, another first in the history of America's National Parks.

It was also the first National Park to be almost completely destroyed by fire. In October 1947, a conflagration that lasted four days destroyed most of the houses on the island and reduced much of its virgin forest to charred stumps. It has been rebuilt, of course, and reforested, but there are still ghosts of the original 18th-century salt-water farms to be discovered along the more than 100 miles of nature trails that wind through the park.

Less adventuresome visitors to the park can drive over 200 miles of roads or 50 miles of bridle paths that are the legacy of John D. Rockefeller, Jr., who built a two-road system, one for carriages and another for saddle horses. But they miss the joys the 19th-century visitors found the best part. They miss the huge lilacs in the spring and the lilies that grow along old forgotten stone walls. They miss biting into a sweet apple from a tree that was once part of a long-forgotten orchard. They miss watching seabirds at work, or watching a deer along the shore of a hidden lake.

And unlike the old summer people, people are experiencing Acadia all year 'round these days. Parts of the park are open in the winter for snowmobiling and cross-country skiing. If the Rockefellers and the Morgans had tasted that pleasure, they might still be there. In spite of the high cost of servants.

Previous pages: boats at Bar Harbor, including (right inset) the luxurious ferry *Bluenose*, which conducts cruises to Yarmouth, Nova Scotia. Founded in 1796, Bar Harbor, on Mount Desert Island's eastern peninsula, was a quiet, secluded fishing village until the mid-1800s, when its charms were recognised first by artists and then by vacationing millionaires who built themselves fine homes and turned the village into a fashionable society resort. This era came to a swift end, however, with the Great Depression and the Great Fire of 1947, which destroyed many of the holiday homes. Yet today the town is once again a lively holiday resort and, retaining the charm of its original seafaring lifestyle, its tranquil harbor (these pages and overleaf) shelters both colorful fishing boats and elegant yachts.

These pages: Bar Harbor, picturing (above) the fishing boat *Northern Miner*, (right and top right) some of the town's charming shops and boutiques, and (facing page) sailing vessels of all shapes and sizes on the blue waters of the harbor.

Situated on the shores of Frenchman Bay, at the foot of Acadia National Park's great mountains, Bar Harbor enjoys a location of breathtaking natural beauty which inspired its first founders to name it Eden. Today, the town's appeallies not only in these surroundings, but also in its own appearance, which is enhanced by fine buildings such as the white, clapboard Congregational Church (left). As the commercial center of Mount Desert Island and a base for visitors to the park, the town also offers all the attractions of a modern resort, including a range of accommodation, a lively nightlife and varied cuisine. The town is in fact renowned for its delicious seafood, which is freshly-caught from the waters around the harbor (previous pages) and cooked to perfection at waterfront restaurants such as The Chart Room (previous pages inset) and the homely Fisherman's Landing (below). Facing page: the 60-foot pleasure boat *Bay Lady II.*

Previous pages: (main picture) the excursion boat *Janet May*, a 64-foot schooner that can carry 50 passengers, (inset left) a rowing boat and fishing floats, and (inset right) the trawler *Northern Miner*, all at Bar Harbor (these pages). Above: an aerial view of the Bar Harbor coastline, looking east towards Winter Harbor on the mainland and picturing the islands lying in Frenchman Bay, including, from left to right, Bar Island, Sheep Porcupine Island, Burnt Porcupine Island, Long Porcupine Island and Bald Porcupine Island. Left: houses nestling in the verdant, leafy woodlands around Bar Harbor. Facing page: (top) the *Mount Katahdin*, one of the many splendid pleasure cruisers operating around the harbor, and (bottom) fir trees silhouetted against the burnished sky of sunset.

Previous pages: an aerial view of the coastline of Bar Harbor, showing part of Bar Island on the right. Left and overleaf right: the First National Bank on Bar Harbor's lively Main Street (these pages and overleaf left).

Previous pages: a yacht moored at Bar Harbor (these pages). Bottom left: the graveyard of the Congregational Church, site of a memorial (facing page) to Eden's Sons, Bar Harbor's Defenders of the Union in the Civil War, (left and bottom) St. Saviour's Episcopal Church, and (below) the Christian Science Society.

Previous pages left: a bronze fountain, (previous pages right) golden autumn leaves and (this page) a bandstand and benches in a restful, shady park in Bar Harbor. Opposite the park is the white weatherboard Bar Harbor Congregational Church (facing page), with its splendid Classical portico and elegant spire reaching towards the summer sky. Overleaf: a dainty, white footbridge leads over a tranquil pond to the Mount Desert Island Museum. It is scenes such as this that illustrate why Bar Harbor, and indeed the whole of Mount Desert Island, has been popular with artists since the mid-19th century.

Facing page: an aerial view of part of the rugged coast of Bar Harbor (these pages), scattered with luxury homes surrounded by lush, green woodland. Left: an aerial view of the town, picturing the Bar Harbor Congregational Church in the left foreground and Main Street on the right, running inland from the harbor. Bar Harbor is a mecca for ship-spotters as its waters are frequently visited by magnificent vessels such as the luxury Viking cruise liner (below). Overleaf: looking east from the summit of Cadillac Mountain.

Right: the slopes of Cadillac Mountain, blanketed by richly-colored vegetation, lead up to a rounded granite summit (facing page) that reaches 1,532 feet above sea level. The ascent to the mountain, beginning just west of Bar Harbor, is one of the most popular routes in Acadia National Park and offers superb views of Eagle Lake to the west and, to the east, Bar Harbor and the islands in Frenchman Bay, which from that height resemble great stepping stones. As well as being Mount Desert Island's highest peak, Cadillac Mountain is also the highest point on the eastern seaboard of the United States, and is thus the first place in North America to be struck by the light of dawn (below and overleaf).

Dark fingers of land and strips of heavy cloud become indistinguishable from each other in fantastic sunsets (these pages) viewed from Cadillac Mountain. Facing page: the view northeast towards the great expanse of Frenchman Bay, and (right) looking west at the sun sinking over Eagle Lake. Overleaf: a very different daytime view from the mountain top, showing the rich colors of the turning leaves, the soft, white clouds scudding across the sky and the brilliant blue of Frenchman Bay. Ranged from left to right are Bar Island, Sheep Porcupine Island, Burnt Porcupine Island and Long Porcupine Island.

Cadillac Mountain was named after the Frenchman, Antoine de la Mothe Cadillac, who was given Mount Desert Island by the governor of Canada during the 17th century. Surprisingly, he chose to spend only a few months on the island then headed west and founded Detroit. Previous pages: (insets) rapture at the breathtaking views from the summit of Cadillac Mountain. Many visitors to Acadia National Park make the effort to climb the mountain in time to see the magic of the rising sun (main picture), whose rays strike the mountain top before reaching anywhere else in the United States. This page: views in the Champlain Mountains, including (facing page) Eagle Lake by day and (left) at sunset. Overleaf: Bear Brook, backed by the stony face of the gorge.

Previous pages: swampy land near Beaver Dam Pond, (these pages) the
rocky coastline around Schooner Head, (overleaf) the southeast
shoreline, and (following pages) Park Loop Road.

Previous pages: (main picture) the rugged eastern coastline of Schooner Head, on which is situated one of Mount Desert Island's many luxury homes (top left inset). Bottom right inset: red foliage growing amongst smooth granite boulders on the southeastern shores, and (remaining insets) rugged stratified rock on the southern coastline. The inland scenery of Acadia National Park is every bit as beautiful as its coast and offers a stunning variety of terrain and vegetation. These pages: slender silver birches growing (left) around Bear Brook and (facing page) along part of the 19-mile-long Park Loop Road. Overleaf: the jewel of the island's eastern coastline, Sand Beach, which is comprised of thousands of tiny seashells.

Previous pages and above: Sand Beach, (top and facing page) the area around Thunder Hole (left), a narrow chasm where at high tide the crashing waves sound like thunder.

One of the best ways to enjoy the magnificent scenery of Acadia National Park's eastern coastline (these pages) is to travel along Ocean Drive (facing page bottom), a part of Park Loop Road that is one-way for eleven miles. For the first few miles the drive winds along the eastern slopes of the Champlain Mountains, then between Sand Beach and Otter Point it hugs the shoreline, affording dramatic views of the crashing waves below and passing sights such as Thunder Hole and the sheer Otter Cliffs, which rise 110 feet above the sea.

Previous pages: the vibrant colors of autumn glimmer on the trees along Park Loop Road. Right: the smooth, reflective waters of Jordan Pond, which is situated at the foot of the cliffs of Penobscot Mountain. One of the park's most beautiful sights, this stretch of water is popular with fishermen as its well-oxygenated waters provide a perfect habitat for lake trout and salmon. Below: an aerial view of the sweeping curve of the harbor (below right and facing page top) of Seal Harbor, a delightful village where yachting is the main activity. Facing page bottom: sunset bejewels the waters of Ingraham Point, on the coast just east of Seal Harbor. Overleaf: yachts and motor boats line a jetty in Northeast Harbor.

Top: the medieval-style gateway to a luxury private home (right) near Northeast Harbor (remaining pictures), whose waters provide shelter for a variety of sailing boats.

Previous pages: Northeast Harbor, on the eastern side of the entrance to Somes Sound. One of the most beautiful of Acadia National Park's tourist centers, this fashionable coastal town is mainly known for its summer yachting events, which include races, regattas and cruises. Among its other attractions are whale watching trips and excursions to the nearby Cranberry Isles, one of which, Little Cranberry Island, is the site of Isleford Historical Museum, where the area's history since 1604 is illustrated and intriguing tales are told of smuggling during the War of 1812. Aerial views (these pages and overleaf) of Northeast Harbor reveal the many grand homes overlooking calm, blue

Previous pages and facing page top: romantic scenes of Somes Sound as the early morning mist rolls over the water. Facing page bottom: Somes Sound by day, and (right) overlooked by the rich russets and flame reds of autumn. This beautiful fjord, dividing Mount Desert Island's two peninsulas, was named after Abraham Somes, who, in 1762, founded Somesville, the island's first permanent settlement, at the sound's northern end. Above: Echo Lake, a large freshwater lake at the foot of Beech Mountain that provides cool, clear water for swimmers and an abundance of salmon and brook trout for fishermen. Overleaf: (main picture and top inset) agricultural land in western Mount Desert Island, and (bottom inset) a forest scene near Indian Point, on the southwestern coastline. Following pages: a lake near Southwest Harbor.

These and previous pages: views of Southwest Harbor. Overleaf: (main picture and bottom inset) Seawall, on the south coast (top inset), near the island's southernmost tip, which is marked by Bass Harbor Head Light (following pages).

Previous pages: Bass Harbor Head Light. Facing page bottom: Bass Harbor Marsh, near Bass Harbor (remaining pictures and overleaf), one of the most unspoilt coastal villages on the island.

Lying southwest of Mount Desert Island is Isle au Haut (right), two thirds of which is part of Acadia National Park. Top right: Mount Western, beyond the village of Bernard (remaining pictures) in the Bass Harbor area (overleaf). Final page: Seawall.